Inspirations

Lawrence Harvey

ISBN: 978-1-6847-1710-1 (sc)
ISBN: 978-1-6847-1709-5 (e)

Because of the dynamic nature of the Internet, any web addresses or links contained in this book may have changed since publication and may no longer be valid. The views expressed in this work are solely those of the author and do not necessarily reflect the views of the publisher, and the publisher hereby disclaims any responsibility for them.

Any people depicted in stock imagery provided by Getty Images are models, and such images are being used for illustrative purposes only. Certain stock imagery © Getty Images.

Lulu Publishing Services rev. date: 01/17/2020

There will always be laughter

In the Spirit of an old religion

The Mystery that will never end begins now

We in the wisdom of our people

Live well

Old souls gather for a celebration

Life is in session

Live and prosper well under the sun

It is good to be here

For goodness

And unconditional love

Today we mourn for our friend

The flowers are laid out

Some friends come to pay their respect

Some remembered a request

The stars didn't fall from the sky The fields

are rich with harvest The river still gives up

its fish The world we imagine is still

Beautiful as if today was yesterday

When life was everything

Your life is changing Because you have

changed From the person you were

To the person you've become

Transformed by love

It is a Miracle of Healing

In my dream

Is you

In your love

You came

Wiped away all

My tears

Gave me love

Everlasting

Encouraged by you

I am

May God test you

In the garden

Of

Your love

Raising little flowers

To

Explore the world

May your prayer

Be heard

By your silence

When the greatest gift

Manifests

In

Your life experiences

Happiness

Came alone sat by

me Then whispered

Something in my ear

Why are you telling me this

My dear Happiness

Because

I love you

The words

That formed out

of My thoughts

Yesterday

Will be heard

Today

A

Beautiful

Presence

Is with us

Just Look

around To

see the

Goodness

A special kind

Of woman

Is unselfish

In all she does

See

How beautiful she is

Someone needs to tell her

How beautiful she is

That beauty and nature

Are one

I salute you

Then

Encourage you

To celebrate

Your life today

While The

day is Still

with you

I think of how

One miracle

Will change the tune

Of everyone

Everywhere

Forever

The knowledge of love

The condition

Being unconditional

The representation

Being the old religion

The hope of tomorrow

Being acted on today

Do I salute you

My friend

Live well

"The Hope of Tomorrow

Being Acted on Today"

There is a strange

Mystery

Hidden in the land

The word that came with

Power and authority

A word I am unable

To speak of

My friend tomorrow may

Never come

I may never see the hope

Of my children

Singing a new song

Let us live

In the

Silence

Of a beautiful

World

In peace

And harmony

I am blessed

To be

In your presence

I am amazed

At how

You make things work.

Blessings are

Yours to have

Then give in return

Why not be a Blessing!

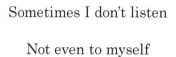

Sometimes I don't listen

Not even to myself

It's in these times

I must give myself a talk

To encourage my own thoughts

It's something else

To encourage yourself

Thoughts

Are Like

Prayers

In The

Silence

Of

The

Day

Going out to

Change the world

There's something

I miss

About you

It is the beauty

I experience

"You in the Beautiful Presence"

How very blessed

Are the people

Who know you

How very blessed

Are the people

Who surround you

In the Beautiful Presence

Her name

Is

Beautiful

Be encouraged

So you

Can

Encourage

Someone else

There are many

Miracles

On this planet

You

Just happen to be

One of them

Did you remember

To pray

For someone today?

Did you pray

For someone

In your family?

Did you pray For

our leaders The

world over?

Do you remember

How to

Love unconditionally?

I'd walk a mile

To pray for you

Then back again

To pray

Some more

Since

There is a God

in heaven Who

looks down On

us

Ask and it shall

Be given

A miracle

Will happen today

As it

Happens every day

Someone will be healed

Someone will live

Stand still

A miracle

Is about to happen

Sky in a sky

Roll back

The time

The sun

Mixed with water

A strange appearance

Came upon

All of Mankind

There is a teacher

Looking

For a student

A student wanting

To learn

The meaning of life

The Miracle that

Is called upon

Your life today

Will echo for

Generations

To come

He

Likes to show off

His

Goodness and Mercy

I thought

The same thoughts

As my teacher

Who gave up

Her imaginations

In exchange for a day

To think the same thoughts

Driven by desire

That changed the Mystery

Into imagination

Once again

Teacher

What is the greatest

Moment in life

The greatest moment

Is the breath

You take

Once that is over You

would have arrived At

your destination

If I had a choice

I'd chose a moon

Inhabited of water and berries

The mystery behind

Each thought

The thought behind

Each imagination

Imagination that imagines

A wonderful silence

That desire above all thought

Issues with the last meditation:

Don't know if I was

in a dreamlike state

or awake

Maybe I need to focus

On listening

Instead of talking so much

One cannot listen if one

Is constantly talking

The issue is the tongue

The music is always met

With pleasure

Desire orders nothing

Has everything Want

was lost long, long

ago

Need is ever present

My heart is only human

The last thought Sent

down from Heaven

Rescued me

I am the only imagination

I know

Sing a beautiful song

Imagine great things

I am the thought that keeps pace

With every beat

Of my heart

In a silent way I am

The Music

I am a dream

That looks into the darkness

Pull out some light

And call it a day

I am restless

Can't seem to be

Who I want to be

Old habits keep chasing

After me

I am love

Yet I have not loved

Myself in a long time

I am imagination What you

think you know Is not what

you know Embrace your

creative self

I am Spirit

Having a human experience

Living in a physical world

My choice

To dream and desire

Other things

That has nothing to do

With life

The road is clear

No sorrow, no pain

There is no sorrow

In our heart of hearts

Must we believe in this

hope That has captured

the Imagination of man

Redeemed us from our Self-destructive ways

Gave us rest at every turn He

gave us rest at every turn No

sorrow, no pain

There is no sorrow

In our heart of hearts

Stand still and be ready

Make way

THE ROAD IS CLEAR

There is nothing left undone

To be done

Make way the road is clear

Be ready to return to the former things

Be ready to return to glory

Surely you believe as I see

The wonder, the inspiration, the choice

The fall and the rise back

To where it all began

You have a problem Now

you have a solution

Choose to listen instead of

Being heard

Take a knee and kiss the sky

Welcome

When I look up and see you

Walking through the door

My mind begins to wonder in appreciation

I get a sense of hope

That someone cares enough for me

That I in return must do the same

You are a miracle

I am glad you're here Have

a seat and rest yourself You

are in for a long journey

As simple as this whole process is

We can complicate things

I know it took me 20 years to get ONE

Even if you don't know it yet

You are in the right place

No one comes into these rooms by mistake

We've been waiting for you

In fact some of us even prayed

We once sat where you are sitting

Thought the same thoughts

Felt the same way

Had the same Legal and Family problems

Why I had such a distorted view of life

I couldn't see the truth

I lived the lie day in and day out

I believed the lie

That things would get better

They never did

One by one I lost

It all

You are in the right place

WELCOME

YOU HAVE TO HAVE PERSONALITY...

Can you channel a thought

Into a thousand hearts While

running the L.A. Marathon Bake

a German Chocolate Cake Swim

to Catalina Island

Flirt with a shark And

hold your breath For

10 seconds

Do you have any personality at all

Can you sing or dance, paint a sunset

Run for Governor, proclaim a holiday

Are you still silly with

Imagination

You have to have Personality

It's not who you hang out with

But how do you feel

When you're in a crowd

Your personality is your identity

Your identity is your makeup

Your makeup is your character

Your character is sometimes humorous

That humor

Comes out of your

PERSONALITY

Need I say more

Have you ever felt like giving up And

the world around you seems lost

Again you find yourself in a hopeless

Situation

Ready to die, despair sets in

As you think of the harm You've

caused yourself and others Not

willing to pick up

The pieces and move forward

Self-pity invites itself to the table

You entertain old ideas

That feeling of being unworthy

Knocks you down

Inside the pit

Of doom and gloom

Yet you are

PERSISTENT

Because HOPE never gives up

Something inside

Stands you to your feet

Dusts you off

Then turns your life around

The choice defined by the motive

Think about it

Are your choices driven by

A hidden motive

That

Self-seeking desire

That got you in the position

You are in now

Separated you From

family and friends Took

over your home

Drove your car and left you

In pain

OH THE PAIN

Do I have your attention

Are you willing to take some

Suggestions

After all

This is a life or death matter

And if you're not ready

I'll understand

No one will force you

Into this deal

You have to want it

More than your desire of anything

Believe that I believe

You are worth saving We

care and will be here For

you

Why don't you

Get you some

Humility

Wrap it up in

Your imagination

Toss it in the

Air

And see what

Happens

FOR ERMA BECAUSE SHE WAS

IN PAIN ONE DAY

Looking into a pair

Of soft brown eyes With

no expression of pain Upon

her face

I saw a beautiful exotic

Woman

Who may have been just

As alone and lonely as I

Through the silent tears

That escaped its outward

Appearance

She captured my imagination

With a glance

As she held back her

Own tears

Mine were flowing with

Ease

Not yet realizing that I couldn't

Help Erma Before I first

examined Myself

Am I old-fashioned

Enough

To love the things

That touch

The heart

That spark

The flame

That lights

The fire

That burns

Eternal

That created

The desire

In the first place

I heard your footsteps

Follow

me To a

Wonderful

Place

Where we

will Meet

Happiness

In a silent

Afternoon

By chance I knew you

I mean

I really knew you

When you were happy

Not that your happiness

Depends upon outward

Conditions

My dear has anyone

Ever told you How

Amazingly beautiful

You are

It was never about me

You are in my dream

You are in my dream

I wonder

Will it ever

Rain

Sitting on a porch

Eating watermelon

Watching the sunset

You in my dream

Imagine Jasmine

and

Sweet orange peels

It is the music that

Played me

Your song

Is all I hear

Amazing isn't it

The song

Coming

Out of

A

Thought

From you

I hear your music with each

New day

Oh how I forget

To remember

That the things in you

Are also in me

You are the music

ME

I'm still learning how to

Sing this song

I will always laugh with your

Laughter

It is the humor that exists

Between us

The laughter of today

Here and now

The happiness we all share

Together

In a private second

When no one is looking

You will remember

IT

One more time

Love is never finished

With you Because it

never stops Loving you

The music never stops

It is a continuous

Vibration

Of the motion

That is you

It is your music

I feel Running

through The

thick of me

Your vibrations

I enjoy Today

And every day I am

With you

Come fill me

With intimacy

Deep

Inside the cave of happiness

I am the

music I hear

Everyday

It is the only

Music

I hear when life

Is in session

The magic I feel in your

Music

Is a tune above

The rest

The joy of last

Summer

A full moon in the

Night

Sing with me my friend

And the music will

Become

You

It's most like home

In the sky

In a

Silent way

In memory of my

Ancestors

Who were a decent

People

I, like the others

Are waiting

For your return...

...FIX IT!

Picture a world in a universe

In the cosmos Waiting

To be discovered

By beings

From another world in the

Universe

The same cosmos

Searching for precious

Metals

To operate a game

On another planet For

an ancient teenage

Ruler

With nothing better to do.

Let your beauty feel the pain

In all the world

You've changed

From the broken that once

Was

To the highest of the

High

It is so very amazing

The Voice of creation.

The great unknown

Is where

I hear your silence

This music of the ages

Fills my soul

I hear a symphony

Between us

It is the great connection

Of the universe

Take me deeper into my memory

Of TODAY.

It is something else like I've

Never seen

The silence that came out

Of a word

From the deepest depth

Of meaning

How very true this mystery

Began

Is it the music I hear

Between the sound

Of your voice

In the silence of your

Minutes

The recipe of life

Surrounds me Sending

imagination into My well-being

With a hint of jasmine

And

Sweet orange peels

This is my song, it is the music

I played throughout my life

It is a song both bitter And

sweet

If you identify with any part of it

Beware

For like me, I played to a different

Drummer

The choices I made were not

Always good

The adventures I had with

Mr. Barleycorn

I shall never forget, for if I do

I just might repeat

That endless cycle of misery

I endured in my practice

I have but one request

It is simple The

music in me

Sings out

I know that joy Comes

with the morning Yes

I have experienced such Joy

Let Us

Encourage

Each

Other

In my imagination is the

Sound of music

I hear the laughter

Within a thousand

Worlds

How ancient are the days

You left behind

A miracle within

A miracle

Still listening...still laughing

It has always been my experience

With you

From the very first day

I was born

Until today

Which I call today

Because

Today like every other

Day

Is the only day that exists

I am not promised

TOMORROW

The secret is in everything

I think I know

Because

Imagination

Desires

The absolute unknown

Am I going to

Desire you

When you desire me

Are your feelings

Going to welcome me

Into your heart

This morning

Or do I have

To pour

A sweet-tasting happiness

Onto your lips

Every minute of the

Hour

I long for you

In a different way

Oh how I wait to see you

Face to face

Every second of every

Minute

I breathe

I am a part of the source

Therefore I am with you

As you are with me

In every breath I take

With every silent moment

I am a poet so I live a poet's

Life

A CONVERSATION WITH SELF

The other day you looked intent

When you spoke of change

Think, this pain comes without

Any thought of change

I only whispered

Isn't it possible that we who have

Been abused can escape the dreams

And nightmares that linger on in our

Every day living

The pain is a constant reminder

Of the hell

We've gone through

It is no longer necessary

To expose myself to the pain

Now

That I find comfort in your words

I'm tired of living in an illusion

That everything is okay When

it's not okay to be abused And

Then turn around and abuse myself

Where innocence is replaced

The tears in your eyes dry up

You can't look straight

For the thought of it happening again

The guilt, the shame, the hurt

The pain, the cross

And the doublecross

Because you trusted them and they betrayed you

How can you TRUST again

I'm afraid to close my eyes and sleep

For fear of someone touching me

HANDS, FACES, FEET, LAUGHTER

The turn of the door handle

Whom can I trust

Where can I turn

What is happening to me

Oh the pain

I find you intense Wanting to

capture my little soul To hold me,

abuse me

Control me with your substance

That I may fly away

The hurt, the shame, the abuse

I'm afraid of who I am You

made me hard, unloving You

justified your actions

I believed you, I trusted you

Now I'm abused and used

The scars Remind

me of this PAIN

I feel every time you breathe

Fear grips me

I'm taken to a room

In my mind and seduced

Of the thoughts I can't escape

If pain is a motivator

Then I should be kicking somebody's

Ass right about now

Move over dream

I'm about to have a nightmare

Pardon me but is that shame

I see on your face

You'd be good to check that at the door

I'm going to let you come in this time

But don't come around here again With

Your long face and looking a mess

Like you rolled over in a barrel

Well speak up, my ears are on

You got something to say?

I hurt and it won't go away

It followed me here Out

of the shadow of my

Experience

It's imagination, the magic

of TODAY

It's about friendship and

fellowship

It's all about happiness

It's about inspiration It's

all about you and the

things you do

It's gentleness and

tenderness

It's all about TODAY

A MOST WONDERFUL THING

The JOY that exists

Between friends Has

emptied the sea Of

its emptiness

Filled it with

Understanding

Compassion

And love

I know

Of a sweet

HAPPINESS

Living In

the

Experience

Of us all

A magic spell

A dream

Move over

My dear

I am not

Ready

For you yet

You speak of magic

As if You

know

What it is

My dear You

are every

Magic moment

I hold in my heart

This magic In

a beautiful

World

Came to believe

In the

Ability to be

Transformed

The choice of another

Wonderful day

There is something else

You need to know My

dear

Listen to your heart

It beats for you

It is a beautiful heart The

beauty of the beautiful

Presence that is you

My dear

You came before I was ready

To take you on this

MAGICAL JOURNEY

I heard your

music It was a soft

Tender melody

With the kindness

Of your heart

Speaking in a song

My dear

Isn't today a good day

To be loved

In a very special way

The music

It came to sit with me

How beautiful her song

May her magic

Never leave my side

Every day

In every way

LOVE, LOVE VIII

The center Of

excitement Is

you

The pleasure

Of giving

Is you

Now the screams

I hear

Are yours

OLD CAN OF SWEET MUSIC

Mr. came to chop down the tree

All the bees

Came after me

Into the woods this old woman

Took flight

Mr. had an old can of sweet music

I saw him from afar

Chopping and chopping

Bees buzzing overhead

Tree fell

Mr. picked up

His can, his wood

Then he left

Without ever

Saying goodbye

MIDNIGHT MAGIC

Midnight magic

Across The

sky Dangling

stars That

caught My

eye

Within

My hand

I held so

Close

You're the magic

THE END OF A BEAUTIFUL DAY

INTIMACY

The

Essence

Of

Intimacy

Can

Change

Your

Heart

Forever

Experience

Took me

By the

Hand

And

Showed

me The

Beautiful

Places

The mystery

in the music

Who is going

To show me

The

Beautiful places

There is

Kindness

In a wonderful

Intimate imagination

That took me

To

A secret place

Hidden in The

magic that Is

you

The shadow

That

Whispered

That

Visited my dream

Invaded

My relationship with sleep

Gave me her Imagination

As if she were

Paradise blue

I placed a rose

On the table

By the place

She would be

A red rose To

remind her Of

me

One more sunset

More beautiful

Than the last

What more can I say

Now that you have

Appeared

Like magic

In a room

There hangs a picture

On the wall

A masterpiece

Of a woman

Who looks like you

It's something else

The beauty

The presence

Above all imagination

Your music

Is divine

I salute the beautiful

Presence in you

In the magic

Of another day The

kindness in you Is

silent

I salute that silence in you

Pray

And see what happens

When

Was the last time

Someone told you

How

Beautifull and special

You are

My dear

Does it ever get old

Waiting

For your soul mate

To appear

It was I who placed

That rose at your feet

I definitely want

To be in Your

presence Away

from the Magic

Of the day

To hear your music

Surrounding me

With kindness

In a dream

I wandered around

Looking for a mirror

Who looks for a mirror

In a dream

Ha-ha-ha

I became silent

For the day is still

Young

I am the story

Talked about

The history

I am told

Both good and bad

So how is it that you

Know more of my story

Than me

I salute you

The God of all comfort

Dear lord may I never

Forget

Your love and mercy

May I always remember

It is you

Who walks beside me

In my most troubled

Days

It is everything

I need

When it moves, I move

It is everything

To me

In a silent day

You came

I salute the God in you

Unconditional

I think

Of You

That way

Someone

Would

Say

When I think of you

I pray

God please help thanks amen

Why do I have

it so Gooooood

Understand I'm not

Complaining

I salute the God

In my friends In

everyone

Amen

I Salute

The

Silence

In

Prayer

Now

See

What

Happens

God please help thanks...amen

FRIENDS

When I was hurting

And in pain

You came by Pulled back

the curtains Of my life

Put on a pot of tea

I talked

And you listened to me

If today is called

today Then what will

Tomorrow bring

A flower in the rain

A stone against the grain

A wheel within a wheel

The joy without the pain

In the chance that

I find you

In the mystery

May we always

Greet each other

I salute the beauty in you

If I had a second chance

I'd meet you for the

Very first time

What would be different

I don't know

The stars didn't say

Destiny will tell its

Own story

There is a higher calling

For

A greater purpose

Live well

My friend

and give of Yourself

The magic of the excitement

That is you

May the special places

In your life excite you May

your joy surround you With

peace

In every direction

As the sun rises so shall

It set then rise again

May your sunrise remind you

Of each sunset

I love you more than

You will ever know

Ahhhhhh

Did you smile just now

I am willing to be loved

Oh beautiful morning

How special was the

Day

June 4th

A little magic opened

My eyes

It was a beautiful

Day

Oh beautiful morning

How very special You

are

The magic Within

this dream It

seems to never

End

The inspiration Excites

the imagination That

creates

The desire

Within

The

Essence

Of

Intimacy

Can

Change

Your

Heart

Forever

Old cans of loneliness

Can never

Take away

the Happiness

Stored

Within

Remember

Life is always in session

Live well

Be content

Don't let anyone

Remove

The joy that is yours

Are your feelings

Going to welcome

Me

Into your

Heart

This morning

Or

Do I have to pour

A Sweet taste of love

Into

Your thoughts

The secret is in everything

I Think

I Know

Because imagination

Desires The

absolute

Unknown

This is my song, it is the music

I played throughout my life

It is a song both bitter and sweet

If you identify with any part of it

Beware

For like me I played to a different

Drummer

The choices I made were not

Always good

The adventures I had with

Larrybarleycorn

I shall never forget, for if I do

I just might repeat

That endless cycle of misery

I endured in my disease

Do we have history

How beautiful it is

With our ancestors

Looking on

How amazing a time

How beautiful you are

Today, Remember

yesterday

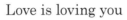

Love is loving you

Never finished

With you

Because it never stopped

The music never stops

It is a continuous

Vibration

Of the motion

That is you

Love is imagination

The music of today

It's about friendship

And happiness

It's about inspiration It's

all about you and the

Things you do

It's gentleness

And tenderness

It's all about today

The only day I know

God please help THANKS

AMEN

Made in the USA
Las Vegas, NV
15 February 2023

67549305R00081